Min Ha'aretz

Making Meaning from Our Food

by Julie Botnick and Becca Linden

Based on work by Judith Belasco, Rabbi Mick Fine,
Dr. Ronit Ziv-Kreger, and Jenna Levy

BEHRMAN HOUSE
www.behrmanhouse.com

Visit www.behrmanhouse.com/min-haaretz for further resources.

Design: Terry Taylor Studio
Project Editor: Ann D. Koffsky
Editorial Consultants: Ellen Rank and Mark Levine

Copyright © 2016 Hazon
Published by Behrman House, Inc.
Springfield, NJ 07081
ISBN 978-087441-938-2
Printed in the United States of America

Library of Congress Cataloging-in-Publication Data

Botnick, Julie, author.

Min Ha'aretz : making meaning from our food / by Julie Botnick and Becca Linden ; based on work by Judith Belasco, Rabbi Mick Fine, Ronit Ziv-Kreger, and Jenna Levy.

pages cm

ISBN 978-0-87441-938-2

1. Food—Religious aspects—Judaism—Juvenile literature. 2. Jews—Food—History—Juvenile literature. [1. Judaism—Customs and practices—Juvenile literature.] I. Linden, Becca. II. Title.

BM729.F66B68 2016

296.7'3—dc23

2015028665

The publisher gratefully acknowledges the following sources of photographs:

(T=top, B=bottom, M=middle, L=left, R=right)
Cover: Ann D. Koffsky (fish, torah); Shutterstock: Catalin Petolea (boy w/ spade), pockygallery (globe), Ivonne Wierink (crate), Konstantin Yolshin (Plate, hallah), Anastacia - azzzya (recycle), Winai Tepsuttinun (bag) Sergey Novkov (boy w/ tomatoes), Sunny studio (hands), Monkey Business Images (girl), Ohn Mar (vegetable drawings), Maks Narodenko (oranges), merrix (notebook)
Interior: Hazon 5; reneesgarden.com 8M; Terry Taylor 17B; Behrman House 20T; Gateways 25B; Katy Allen 35; Rabbi Fred Scherlinder Dobb 35; Orthodox Union 38; Star-K 38; Fair Trade USA 38; United States Department of Agriculture 38; Rinat Gilboa 60; Wikimedia Commons: R. Kook 35; Maimo 35; Brenda Putnam 38T; Nachmanidies 38M; Master of James 43T; Providence Litho company 47; Gerard Hoet 50; Shutterstock: Framing text Preto Perola; Food fact DVARG; ANCH Toc; Sunny studio 4TL; Dream 79TR; PHOTOCREO Michal Bednarek 6; Petr Svoboda 7M; Maks Narodenko 7L; apiguide 7TR; Monkey Business Images 8T; Paleka BR; Andrii Gorulko 9T; Aigars Reinholds 9B; Kletr 10; Pattanawit Chan 11T; AlexandreNunes 11B; Iryna Rasko 12; Dirk Ercken 13; strelka 14T; bread rolls Studio KIWI 14B; Kazlouski Siarhei 15; shyshak roman16T; Binh Thanh Bui 16M; SeDmi16B; Zeljko Radojko17T; M. Unal Ozmen 17B; S1001 18TL; Guy Burshtein18R;vita pakhai18M; Giuseppe Parisi 19; Katerina Maksymenko 20BL; Madlen 20BR; Nataliya Arzamasova 21; kaband 22BL; CGissemann 22BR; datesbaibaz 23T; Nattika 23BR; matin 23BL; Anna Kucherova 24; Pixel Bunneh 25T; blueeyes 27; Cvijun28-29; Chawalit Pimchan 30; gguy 31T; Nate Allred 31B; smereka 32T; Johnny Adolphson 32B; Kharkhan Oleg 33T; family at table Spotmatik Ltd 34; Lena Pan 36T; Roman Sigaev 36B; Serjio7437M; Edward Westmacott 37T; Tsekhmister 37B; Ruslan Kuzmenkov 40TL; Lenor Ko 40RM; D7INAMI7S 40BL; Christopher Gardiner 40BR; juice topnatthapon 41; label Image Maker 41; D7INAMI7S 41TL; mayakova 41BL; Lenor Ko 41BM; topseller 41BR; bread Africa Studio 41; pears D7INAMI7S 41; Luiz Rocha 42; RonTech3000 43B; Dmitry Naumov 43L; BlueSkyImage 44T; Glovatskiy 44B; Asier Romero 45T; Elena Elisseeva 45B; Sarah2 46; photka 48B; Zurijeta 48T; Radiokafka 49; Max Topchii 52B; Horiyan 52T; Merkushev Vasiliy 53; Patty Orly 54T; Andrei Verner 54B; Winai Tepsuttinun 55T; LoopAll 55BL; Monkey Business Images 55BR;135pixels 57; Zurijeta 58; Jacek Chabraszewski 59; ElenaShow 61; Winston Link 62L; 110655719 62M;bernashafo 62R; Romiana Lee 63; Danylo Kamianskoi 65B; CebotariN 65T; Kamira 66; Pressmaster 67T; sunabesyou 67B; Seregam 68T; Oleksiy Mark 68B; Africa Studio 69; rangizzz 70T; Robyn Mackenzie 70B

Acknowledgements
Min Ha'aretz builds on the work of many staffers and volunteers since the launch of Hazon's first community-supported agriculture program in 2004. We gratefully acknowledge many by name. But if we have missed you, we apologize. Let us know, and we'll add your name to the next edition.

For two of the best readers during early drafts, thank you to Rachel Jacoby Rosenfield and Elisheva Urbas.
For your support from inception to today, thank you to Gayle Adler, Natasha Aronson and her fellow educators at Beit Rabban, Cheryl Cook, David Franklin, Lauren Greenberg, Dr. Mirele Goldsmith, Dr. Aaron Gross, Dr. Steven Lorch, Benjamin Mann, Elan Margulies, David Rendsburg, Nigel Savage, Elena Sigman, Lisa Sjostrom, Liz Traison, and Molly Weingrod.

We are immensely grateful to our terrific editors Ann Koffsky and Dena Neusner at Behrman House.

Hazon's Jewish food work has been supported by generous funders. We are especially grateful to the Covenant Foundation, which supported the original work of Min Ha'aretz, and to the Lippman Kanfer Foundation for Living Torah. This book is dedicated to all the teachers who first piloted and planted these ideas.

Contents

Introduction

- *What foods should I eat or not eat, and why?*

- *How does food connect me to my family and those who came before me?*

- *How does being Jewish enable me to be a steward of the earth?*

These are just some of the questions that *Min Ha'aretz* is about. The words **min ha'aretz** literally mean "from the earth." They're the last two words of the blessing one says before eating bread: *"hamotzi lechem min ha'aretz."* And that blessing is just the tip of the iceberg of two thousand years of Jewish food traditions. When you make *Hamotzi* or *Kiddush* (the blessing over bread or wine), or celebrate a Passover seder, or fast on Yom Kippur, or keep kosher (however you and your family keep kosher), you're connecting Jewish tradition with the food we eat and the choices we make.

Min Ha'aretz is intended to help you learn about some of these issues. Every food choice we make has an impact not only on our bodies, but also on our family, friends, and communities; on the soil from which food grows and the people who grow it; on animals and on ecosystems.

Where does our food come from? Where does our waste go? What issues should we take into account when we make food choices? These questions are Jewish questions and they are also human questions—issues that all of us need to address.

So I hope that you will enjoy *Min Ha'aretz*. And most of all, I hope that you, your friends and families, and indeed all of us will be blessed to eat good food, in good communities—and in eating well, we will make a better world for all.

Nigel Savage,
Founder and President, Hazon

To Grow
Planting Seeds

Where does our food come from? In Jewish tradition, the first people, Adam and Eve, didn't have to farm or work at all to get food. They lived in the Garden of Eden, which was full of ripe fruits and vegetables.

Today, we have a very different reality. Vegetables and fruits start as seeds and go on an amazingly complex journey before they reach our stomachs. Although we have to put more work into growing food than Adam and Eve did, through our work, we become partners with God as protectors of the earth—*shomrei adamah.*

What questions do you have about what it means to be a protector of the earth?

_____

_____

Where Does Food Come From?

Draw a comic strip that illustrates the process of how your favorite food goes from farm to table. For example, the first panel might be a seed, and the last panel your plate (depending on what your favorite food is!). As you move through the panels, think about all the people and places involved in developing that food.

Framing the Text

Food from Seeds

In the first book of the Torah, Genesis, we read that God creates the world. God begins with the heavens and the earth, and ends with the creation of humankind. The chapter also describes the food God gives people to eat.

> God said, "See, I give you every seed-bearing plant that is upon all the earth, and every tree that has seed-bearing fruit; they shall be yours for food." (Genesis 1:29)

Food Fact:

This verse is often quoted by those who wish to illustrate the Torah's support for vegetarianism. (However, the Torah later adds animals to the list of appropriate foods for humans.)

What foods do we eat that are not seed-bearing, and where do those foods come from?

_____

_____

Why do you think the Torah specified that people should only eat seed-bearing foods, and not animals or man-made foods?

_____

_____

_____

_____

Seed Packet Exploration

Each tiny seed contains its own nutritious food supply for a plant to draw on until it is large enough to begin making its own food. The seedling's roots push down into the soil to anchor the new plant and absorb water, and its stem pushes up to get energy from the light. Through the process of photosynthesis, that energy is converted into food for the plant. Farmers and gardeners use numerous techniques to nurture seeds and foster this natural process.

Rainbow Sherbet Watermelons
Yellow Doll F1, New Orchid F1, Tiger Baby F1

MATURE HEIGHT 68 - 80 days	
DAYS TO GERMINATE 7 - 10 days	
SPACE SEEDS 4 inches	
PLANTING DEPTH 1 inch	
SUN/SHADE Full sun	
PLANT IN April – June	

STARTING SEEDLINGS OUTDOORS
Melons need full sun, rich soil and warm temperatures. Plant only when weather is warm and night temperatures stay above 50°. Make slightly rounded hills 2 feet in diameter and 5 feet apart. Sow 5 or 6 seeds 1 inch deep in a small circle on top of each hill. When seedlings have several sets of leaves, **Be Sure To** thin to the 3 strongest plants in each hill.

TO START EARLY INDOORS
No more than several weeks before last frost date, sow seeds in individual pots of seed starting mix. Keep warm and moist, and provide a strong light source until weather warms enough to transplant outdoors (see above).

GROWING NOTES
Amend soil well with aged manure or compost. If summers are short or cool, put down black plastic to retain heat, then plant into holes made in plastic. Where insects are a problem, cover seedlings with floating row covers to exclude them, removing when plants blossom. Keep young vines well watered and fed, tapering off as fruits ripen up for best sweet flavor.

HARVEST AND USE
Pick melons when the tendril closest to the fruit turns brown, and the light patch on the bottom of the melon changes from cream to tan. These small fruitful watermelons keep well in the refrigerator, even after being cut open. You can cut juicy wedges of all 3 colors for summer parties and picnics.

What does the seed packet tell you about how often people need to be involved in the process of growing fruit?

_____

_____

_____

Framing the Text

To Till and to Tend

In Genesis, there are two tellings of the creation story. In the first telling, people are created last. In the second version, people are created first, and only after humankind exists do the rest of the creatures come into being. Because humans are first in this telling, they are like older siblings to the rest of Creation and are given the responsibility of taking care of everything created after them.

> God took the man and placed him in the Garden of Eden, to till it and tend it. (Genesis 2:15)

Food Fact:

There is a Jewish legend that the pomegranate has exactly 613 seeds, the number of *mitzvot,* or commandments, in the Torah.

What are you responsible for in your home or school? Is it your job to take care of anything besides yourself?

_____

_____

_____

What does it mean to tend something for someone, in contrast to "owning" it?

_____

_____

_____

Takeaway It takes a lot of work and many hands to get food from seed to harvest. Though most of us no longer grow our own food, since we all eat and all benefit from the plants and animals around us, we are all responsible for being *shomrei adamah*, protectors of the earth.

To Grow
Caring for the Land

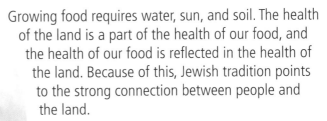

Growing food requires water, sun, and soil. The health of the land is a part of the health of our food, and the health of our food is reflected in the health of the land. Because of this, Jewish tradition points to the strong connection between people and the land.

The Torah commandment of *sh'mitah* is the best example of this: the people are instructed to let the land lie fallow (no planting or harvesting for one year) every seven years. *Sh'mitah* emphasizes that while the land ultimately belongs to God, it is still the people's responsibility to take care of it.

Investigating Sustainability

What is sustainability? A sustainable world is one in which humans and nature exist in harmony while meeting our current and future needs. Maintaining the health of agricultural lands is one way of making sure the earth can provide for generation after generation. People who came before you made conscious choices that made the earth around you look the way it does, for better or worse. You, too, have the power to shape the way the earth looks for people who come after you.

One day Choni Hame'agel was journeying on the road and saw an older man planting a carob tree.

Choni asked, "How long does it take for this tree to bear fruit?"

The man replied, "Seventy years."

Shocked, Choni said, "Do you think you will live another seventy years and be able eat the fruit of this tree?"

The man answered, "I found ready-grown carob trees in the world; as my forefathers planted those for me, so I too plant these for my children." (Talmud, Ta'anit 23a)

How old will you be seventy years from today? Do you think this a long time away? Why or why not?

_____

_____

Name something your grandparent may have done that you still benefit from today.

_____

What do you think your neighborhood would look like if no one planted for the future? Draw your answer in the space below.

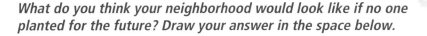

Our Place on Earth

From where we stand, the earth seems really big! Even if we are looking out from the top of a high building on a clear day, we can see, at most, a few miles away. It takes hours, even by plane, just to get from one end of the United States to the other.

But when we think about it more deeply, the earth is actually quite small in relation to the universe. And the amount of land available for living, working, and growing food is actually tiny when compared to the surface of the whole planet.

Pick up an apple. The apple represents the earth.

Take the apple and divide it into four equal pieces.

Place three of the four pieces aside. These represent the 70 percent of the earth's surface that is underwater. The remaining piece represents the portion that is land.

Divide this "land" piece into halves. Set aside one half. This represents land that is too cold, too hot, too dry, or too mountainous, for human habitation. The remaining half represents the portion of the land that is suitable for human habitation.

Take this "human habitation" piece and divide it into four equal pieces.

Set aside three of the four pieces. These represent human occupied areas that are unsuitable for agriculture, such as highways, cities, areas of poor soil, etc. The remaining piece represents the portion of the earth (1/32) that is suitable for agriculture.

On this piece of earth grows all the food eaten by the people of the world. Each year, because of climate change, deforestation, and human settlement, this piece grows smaller.

Sh'mitah, the Torah's Radical Sustainability Decree

Read the following texts about *sh'mitah*, then discuss the questions below.

> God spoke to Moses on Mount Sinai, "Speak to the Israelite people and say to them: 'When you come into the land that I assign to you, the land shall observe a Sabbath for God. Six years you may sow your field and six years you may prune your vineyard and gather in the yield. But in the seventh year the land shall have a Shabbat of complete rest, a Shabbat for God....'"

> "And should you ask, 'What are we to eat in the seventh year, if we may neither sow nor gather in our crops?' I will ordain my blessings for you in the sixth year, so that it shall yield a crop sufficient for three years." *Leviticus, 25:1–4, 20–21*

What questions do you have about sh'mitah?

_____

_____

What do you think a "Shabbat for God" means?

_____

_____

Sh'mitah: For Better or Worse?

In the *sh'mitah* or sabbatical year, the Torah commands that the land in Israel lie fallow. In the long term some claim that this creates healthier farmland and a more sustainable society. But in the short term, it can lead to people losing money and having fewer food options—or even hunger if the year is not properly planned for. Some rabbis have arranged for the *sh'mitah* laws to be relaxed because it is so difficult in the short term, while other rabbis have argued that we cannot lose sight of the importance of sustainability in the long term. Today, some farmers in Israel continue to observe *sh'mitah,* while others do not.

Divide into two groups: one group in favor of sh'mitah, *the other against it. Afterward, have a representative from each group present their list of pros or cons to the class.*

Pro *sh'mitah*	Anti *sh'mitah*
1.	1.
2.	2.
3.	3.

What problems do you think sh'mitah *was meant to solve? What problems do you think* sh'mitah *causes when practiced?*

_____

_____

_____

How can letting the land have a Shabbat change our relationship to the land?

_____

_____

_____

In your opinion, is sh'mitah *a practice that should be adopted today? Why or why not?*

_____

_____

SUSTAINABILITY

Takeaway The laws of *sh'mitah* teach us that we have a responsibility to sustain and take care of the earth. Imagine what the world would be like if no one before us had taken care of it! We can all make changes in our lives, big and small, to ensure that those who come after us will also be able to enjoy the earth.

To Harvest
Our Daily Bread

Bread is a central holy food in Jewish tradition. On Shabbat and holidays, challah is a focus of festive meals, and even during the week bread has an honored place at the table. In Jewish law, bread is the key food that defines a meal as a meal (as opposed to just a snack) and is recognized as a daily connecting point between us, the earth, and Jewish tradition.

Framing the Text

God and Bread

Rabbi Moshe of Kobrin said once to his disciples: "Do you want to know where God is?" He took a piece of bread from the table, showed it to everybody and said: "Here is God."

(From *God in Search of Man* by Abraham Joshua Heschel)

Why do you think Rabbi Moshe chose a piece of bread to hold instead of another food? What about bread makes it different from other options that might have been on his table, such as an apple or an egg?

_____

_____

_____

What do you think Rabbi Moshe of Kobrin thinks the connection is between bread and God?

_____

_____

_____

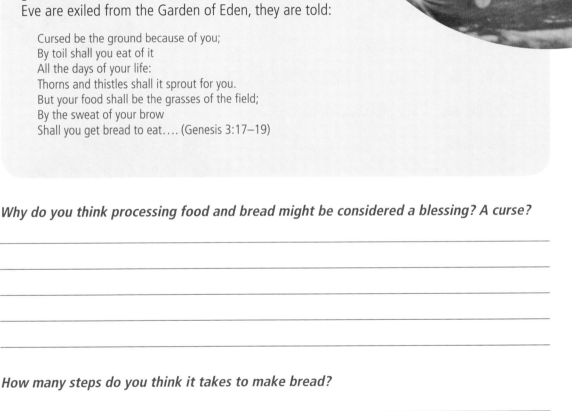

Framing the Text

Is Bread a Blessing or a Curse?

Since bread does not simply grow from the ground ready to eat, like an orange or a tomato, Jewish tradition views it as the result of a blessed partnership: God creates the wheat, and humans harvest that wheat and turn it into bread.

However, that process can often be so challenging to humans that in one case the Torah describes having to grow and make our own food as a curse! When Adam and Eve are exiled from the Garden of Eden, they are told:

> Cursed be the ground because of you;
> By toil shall you eat of it
> All the days of your life:
> Thorns and thistles shall it sprout for you.
> But your food shall be the grasses of the field;
> By the sweat of your brow
> Shall you get bread to eat…. (Genesis 3:17–19)

Why do you think processing food and bread might be considered a blessing? A curse?

_____

_____

_____

_____

_____

How many steps do you think it takes to make bread?

_____

From Wheat Berry to Bread

Working in pairs, try to number the following bread-making steps in the right order.

☐ Separate the wheat kernel (wheat berry) from the stalk.

☐ Store the wheat berries as they are harvested.

☐ Let the dough rise for a few hours.

☐ Plow the land to make sure the soil is soft and loose.

☐ Pull weeds to allow room for the plants to grow.

☐ Cut down the stalks.

Grains of wheat

☐ Mix water and yeast together.

☐ Make sure the soil is moist and healthy with nutrients.

☐ Provide adequate water (but not too much).

☐ Plant seeds.

☐ Add sugar, salt, and flour.

☐ Enjoy your bread.

☐ Provide protection from pests and predators (bugs).

☐ Grind the wheat berries, either at a processing center or by hand, to make flour.

☐ Bake the dough.

Besides bread, what other foods do you eat that are made with flour?

_____

_____

Try This: Making Flour

Step 1: Pour approximately half a cup of wheat berries into a coffee grinder. (Depending on the size of the machine, this amount might need to be adjusted.)

Step 2: Turn the grinder on. You will hear a loud grinding noise, and then the sounds will get softer and softer. The quieter it gets, the closer the wheat berries are to becoming flour.

Step 3: Once the noise is very soft, turn the grinder off and remove your freshly made flour.

Step 4: Use the flour for any recipe that calls for it, such as challah or cookies.

Since you used the entire wheat berry, the flour you just made is called whole wheat flour. If you had chosen to remove the bran and endosperm before grinding the berries, then you would have made white, refined flour.

What did you notice about the transformation you just witnessed?

_____

_____

_____

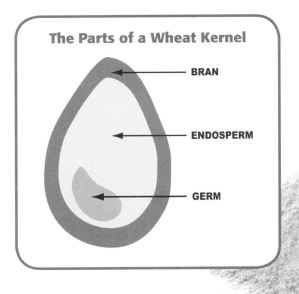

The Parts of a Wheat Kernel

BRAN

ENDOSPERM

GERM

Jewish Bread: Challah!

The foods that Jews around the world include on their Shabbat or holiday tables vary widely. A Shabbat meal in Poland might have potato kugel, while one in Japan could feature sushi. But the one thing that many Jewish meals across the globe have in common is the Jewish bread called challah.

In Jewish tradition, the blessing for eating bread recognizes that people do not obtain their meals solely through their own efforts:

Baruch atah, Adonai Eloheinu, Melech ha'olam, hamotzi lechem min ha'aretz.
Praised are You, Adonai our God, Ruler of the world, who brings forth bread from the earth.

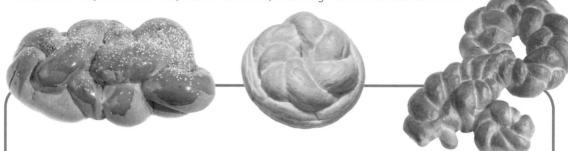

Circle the challah facts you find most intriguing. Underline an idea you would like to try in your home this year.

- The challah we eat is usually braided with three, four, six, or even eight strands. Each of these numbers is symbolic. Six strands, for example, represent the six weekdays, and weaving them together into one loaf of challah represents harnessing their energy and focusing toward the seventh day, Shabbat.

- For Rosh Hashanah, round loaves of challah remind us that the opportunity for renewal always comes around again.

- On the Shabbat after Passover, challah is baked into the shape of a key or baked with an actual key inside! This symbolizes our hope that the gates of prosperity will be unlocked for us, as they were opened for the Jewish people when they entered Israel after leaving Egypt.

- Bird-shaped challah, usually baked before Yom Kippur, represents God's protection of us and the hope that our prayers will soar to the heavens.

- On Shavuot, when we commemorate receiving the Torah at Mt. Sinai, many bake challah into the shape of the tablets of the Ten Commandments.

Making Bread

Today, like Shimon Ben Zoma in the text below, most of us do not make our own bread.

> Shimon Ben Zoma said: How hard it was for Adam to get bread! He had to plow, plant, reap, make piles, thresh, winnow, select, grind, sift, knead, and bake before he could eat. I find all of these done for me! (Talmud, *Berachot* 58a)

Where does your bread come from? Have you ever made bread or challah? Share your experience.

_____

_____

_____

If you were making your own challah and could form it into the shape of something important in your own life, what shape would you make? Draw your answer below.

Takeaway The bread we eat is the product of a journey that requires much human effort, which can be challenging! But bread also reminds us of Jewish tradition's unique perspective that people are in partnership with God.

To Harvest
Jewish Food Around the World

Think about the last food you ate. Where did that food come from? If it was a strawberry, it might have come from Chile. If it was quinoa, it might have come from Bolivia. Did you have a cup of apple juice? You might have tasted a combination of apples from as far away as Chile, China, New Zealand, and Poland.

In all of those countries, there also are Jews. The Jewish people have spread out all over the world. Living in different countries around the world, they used local foods to make the cuisine we now think of as "Jewish food." By experiencing different Jewish foods, we can trace the Jewish people's journeys across continents and centuries.

Name examples of Jewish foods that you have eaten.

_____

_____

_____

What do you think makes these foods "Jewish"?

_____

_____

_____

Framing the Text

Mitzvah or Not?

During the Passover seder we eat *charoset*, a blend of fruits, nuts, wine, and spices.

The Talmudic passage below discusses an interesting disagreement about *charoset*.

> [Eating *charoset*] is not a mitzvah [commandment]. If it is not obligatory, why is it used? Rabbi Ami said: "To neutralize [the taste of the bitter herbs]."
>
> [However,] Rabbi Elazar ben Rabbi Tzadok said: "It is a mitzvah." What religious purpose can it serve?...Rabbi Yochanan said: "It serves as a remembrance of the mortar the Israelites were compelled to prepare when in bondage in Egypt." (Talmud, *Pesachim* 116a)

Do you think eating can be a religious act?

_____

_____

Do you like the taste of charoset? *Does it make you think of bondage or freedom—or something else?*

_____

_____

Are there any foods that remind you of something from your own life? What are they?

_____

_____

Charoset: One Food, Many Recipes.

Differences in Jewish foods arose because Jews in different countries used the ingredients that grew closest to them. With Jewish people cooking all over the world, there is a huge diversity of Jewish foods. *Charoset* is a perfect example. It is made differently around the world.

For each recipe below, paste or draw one ingredient you see in this recipe that is unique to that part of the world.

Venetian *Charoset*

Many Jews visited and worked in Venice, Italy, beginning in the twelfth century CE. At its peak, in the mid-1600s, the Venetian ghetto (where the Jews were forced to live) housed about 3,000 people. Today, the ghetto is still the center of Jewish life in Venice.

10 ounces dates, chopped
12 ounces figs, chopped
½ cup white raisins
¼ cup dried apricots
chopped grated rind of one orange
1½ cups chestnut paste

½ cup pine nuts
½ cup chopped walnuts
½ cup chopped almonds
1½ tablespoons poppy seeds
½ cup wine
honey

Combine all ingredients, gradually adding just enough wine and honey to make the mixture bind. Other Italian charoset recipes include mashed bananas, apples, hard-boiled eggs, crushed matzah, pears, and lemon.

Moroccan *Charoset*

Jews settled in Morocco after the destruction of the Second Temple in 70 CE. After the founding of the State of Israel in 1948, many of Morocco's 265,000 Jews immigrated to Israel and France.

1¾ cups dates
1¾ cups dried figs
½ cup raisins
¼ cup wine

1 cup almonds
2 tablespoons sugar
1 teaspoon cinnamon
½ teaspoon nutmeg

Pit and chop dates, and chop figs. Then place it all in the food processor and blend into a paste. Optional: roll *charoset* into little balls to serve.

Ashkenazi Apple-Nut *Charoset*

Ashkenazic Jews trace their lineage back to the medieval Jewish communities of Germany and France.

2 Granny Smith apples
2 cups almonds, chopped
½ cup sweet wine
1½ teaspoons cinnamon

Peel, core, and dice apples. Chop nuts into slightly smaller pieces than the apples. Add wine and cinnamon; adjust quantities to taste.

Israeli *Charoset*

Jews have immigrated to Israel from a wide variety of countries, including the former Soviet Union, France, the United States, Ethiopia, and India.

2 apples, chopped
6 bananas, mashed
1 lemon, grated and juiced
1 orange, grated and juiced
1¼ cups dates, chopped
1 cup wine

4 teaspoons candied orange
   peel, chopped
1 cup walnuts, chopped
matzah meal
cinnamon
sugar

Mix the fruits, nuts, and wine. Add as much matzah meal as the mixture will take and still remain soft. Add cinnamon and sugar to taste. Mix well and chill before serving.

What, if anything, seems Jewish to you about these recipes?

_____

_____

List five ingredients that you see in the recipes above that you can find locally in your area.

Food Fact:

1. _____

2. _____

3. _____

Local food is defined as food grown within a day's drive away.

4. _____

5. _____

Can an ingredient or food be both Jewish and local?

_____

Create your own recipe for charoset. *What do you want it to taste like? Do you want it to be sweet to balance the bitter herbs, or do you want it to resemble mortar? Or, would you like it to do both?*

Charoset

Recipe By: _____

_____

_____

_____

_____

_____

_____

_____

Takeaway Jewish foods, like *charoset*, are eaten by Jews all around the world, uniting us. But the ingredients used to make these foods vary among countries and cultures based on historical availability and traditions that have been passed down from generation to generation.

Ask your family: Where do your own holiday recipes come from?

Before our food reaches our tables, it starts in another place—as close as our backyard gardens or as far away as Israel or China. Growing food in different climates and sending it around the world ensures that people can have fresh fruits and vegetables all year long. Our food can also connect us to special places; for example, biting into a date might remind us of Israel.

However, there are some downsides to food traveling long distances. Farmers have to pick fruits and vegetables before they are ripe with flavor and nutritional value. Shipping foods across the world produces greenhouse gases that contribute to global climate change. In contrast, foods that are grown locally tend to be fresher because they are grown in-season and reach the consumer more quickly. The distance that food travels from its source to the table is known as *food miles.*

Jewish Traditions and Food Miles

Jewish tradition is strongly linked to food and food rituals. List some of the foods associated with the holidays below. Then note to what extent those foods or their ingredients can be grown near to where you live.

Holiday	Traditional Foods	Local?
Rosh Hashanah		
Sukkot		
Hanukkah		
Tu BiShevat		
Passover		
Shavuot		

These and These

What can we do when our Jewish values conflict with one another? For example, there is the value of celebrating holidays in a traditional way, and also the value of not wasting—*bal tashchit.* On Sukkot, our values suggest that we should shake the *lulav* and *etrog.* But it's not possible to find local, sustainable citrus fruits in most parts of the world. So, in order for us to get an *etrog,* it is necessary to use vehicles, such as trucks and airplanes, to ship it to us. This, in turn, will cause more pollution. How can we resolve conflicts like this? How should we weigh opposing values?

The following sources are often interpreted to mean there is no one right answer when values come into conflict. In fact, there is another Jewish value of having multiple truths at the same time!

> These and these are the words of the living God. (Talmud, *Eruvin* 13b)

> There are seventy faces to the Torah. (Midrash, Numbers *Rabbah* 13:15–16)

Print out your region's local food guide. (You can find the link to some on www.behrmanhouse.com/min-haaretz). Circle the foods you like most. Are there foods you like that are never grown in your region?

_____

_____

Why might it be important to get foods from other places, even if they are far away?

_____

_____

Has there ever been a time in your life when you had two important things to take care of at once? Describe the situation and how you resolved it. How did you balance competing values?

_____

_____

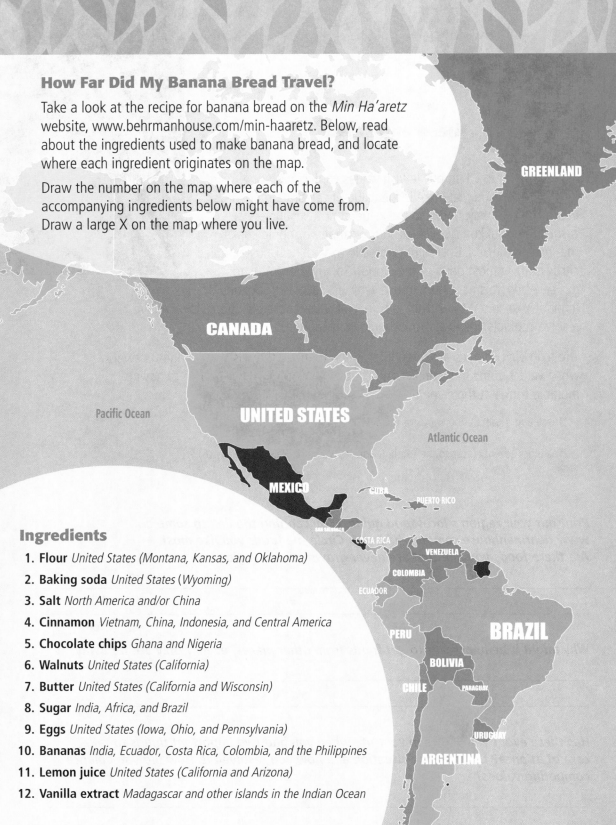

How Far Did My Banana Bread Travel?

Take a look at the recipe for banana bread on the *Min Ha'aretz* website, www.behrmanhouse.com/min-haaretz. Below, read about the ingredients used to make banana bread, and locate where each ingredient originates on the map.

Draw the number on the map where each of the accompanying ingredients below might have come from. Draw a large X on the map where you live.

GREENLAND

CANADA

Pacific Ocean

UNITED STATES

Atlantic Ocean

MEXICO

CUBA

PUERTO RICO

SAN SALVADOR

COSTA RICA

VENEZUELA

COLOMBIA

ECUADOR

PERU

BRAZIL

BOLIVIA

CHILE

PARAGUAY

URUGUAY

ARGENTINA

Ingredients

1. **Flour** *United States (Montana, Kansas, and Oklahoma)*
2. **Baking soda** *United States (Wyoming)*
3. **Salt** *North America and/or China*
4. **Cinnamon** *Vietnam, China, Indonesia, and Central America*
5. **Chocolate chips** *Ghana and Nigeria*
6. **Walnuts** *United States (California)*
7. **Butter** *United States (California and Wisconsin)*
8. **Sugar** *India, Africa, and Brazil*
9. **Eggs** *United States (Iowa, Ohio, and Pennsylvania)*
10. **Bananas** *India, Ecuador, Costa Rica, Colombia, and the Philippines*
11. **Lemon juice** *United States (California and Arizona)*
12. **Vanilla extract** *Madagascar and other islands in the Indian Ocean*

Which ingredient traveled the farthest to reach you? Which traveled the least?

_____

Think about the last meal you ate. Can you name the places where any of the ingredients came from?

_____

_____

⭐ **Takeaway** There is not one correct answer to any of the questions that were brought up in this lesson. It may be that sometimes you eat local food, and sometimes you indulge in non-local foods for special occasions.

Judaism contains rich and diverse traditions about how we should relate to animals. Even though some texts may seem to point in opposite directions, one thing is clear: our texts express deep concern about treating animals with respect. Compassion toward animals is referred to as *tza'ar ba'alei chayim* (literally, "[do not cause] suffering to living beings").

Framing the Text

Compassion for Animals

Jewish tradition tells us that we should not view animals as created only for the sake of human pleasure. Yet, at the same time, Jewish law has authorized the killing of animals to produce meat and other goods that people desire. How do we reconcile these two ideas? Rabbi Yehudah Hanasi, the Talmud teaches, struggled with this question and changed his ways over the course of his life.

Rabbi Yehudah Hanasi was sick for many years, but he was cured, as he had become ill, through a strange happening.

He was once walking to the house of study, when a calf, which was being driven to slaughter, broke loose, came up to the rabbi, buried its head in the folds of the rabbi's clothes, and wept, appearing to plead with him to save it from death. The rabbi said to the calf: "Go to your fate, for to this end you were created." At this, a heavenly voice proclaimed that, as the rabbi had not had compassion on one of God's creatures, he himself should be punished with physical suffering.

For thirteen years the holy rabbi suffered with pain. Then one day he was healed just as suddenly. It happened like this:

A maidservant in the rabbi's house was cleaning a room when she found some newly born weasels. She wanted to put them out of the house, but the rabbi restrained her. "God has compassion on all creatures," he said, "and human beings must follow God's example. Leave the baby weasels in the house." A heavenly voice at once proclaimed that, just as the rabbi had compassion on God's creatures, so should compassion be taken on him. He was immediately cured. (Adapted from the Talmud, *Bava Metzi'a* 85a)

In this story, Rabbi Yehudah Hanasi acted both with indifference and compassion toward animals. Can you list some examples of ways that people behave similarly today?

With compassion	With indifference
1.	1.
2.	2.
3.	3.

Has there been a time in your life when an animal seemed to ask you for help? How did you respond?

_____

_____

_____

_____

Framing the Text

Eating Animals

Eating meat is a complicated issue. In the Torah we see that the controversy goes as far back as creation itself. In the first creation story, in Genesis 1, God prohibits the eating of animals, and gives Adam and Eve only plants to eat.

> God said, "See, I give you every seed-bearing plant that is upon all the earth, and every tree that has seed-bearing fruit; they shall be yours for food." (Genesis 1:29)

Then, after the great flood that takes place at the time of Noah, God gives Noah and his sons permission to eat animals:

> "The fear and the dread of you shall be upon all the beasts of the earth and upon all the birds of the sky—everything with which the earth is astir—and upon all the fish in the sea; they are given into your hand. Every creature that lives shall be yours to eat; as with the green grasses, I give you all these. You must not, however, eat flesh with its life-blood in it." (Genesis 9:2–4)

Why do you think eating animals was permitted for Noah, but forbidden for Adam and Eve? What changed?

_____

_____

_____

Do you think any responsibilities come along with the permission to eat animals? If yes, what are they? If not, why not?

_____

_____

_____

_____

_____

Framing the Text

Animals from Factory Farms

Today, most animals that are grown for food live on industrial farms. Chickens raised for eggs are often kept in cramped cages their entire lives, never seeing sunlight. Many chickens raised for meat have been bred to grow so large so fast, they have trouble even walking without pain. Cattle naturally eat grass, but most cattle today are fed a diet of grains for the last few months of their lives. This makes them gain weight quickly but also makes them sick.

These conditions are unlike anything the ancient rabbis could have imagined, and in fact, the rabbis of the Talmud articulated several guidelines for maintaining humane conditions for animals:

> Do not buy an animal before buying food for that animal to eat. (Jerusalem Talmud, *Ketubot* 4:8)

> You must not sit down to your own meal before you have fed your pets and barnyard animals. (Talmud, *Berachot* 40a)

> When an animal must be killed for food, it must be done in such a way that the pain to the animal is as little as possible. (Talmud, *Bava Metzi'a* 31a–32b)

Most of the Talmud's guidelines are about how to care for animals rather than how to eat them. Why do you think the Talmud focuses on that?

_____

_____

_____

If the rabbis of the Talmud were to write new guidelines today, what do you think they would be?

_____

_____

_____

The vast majority of meat, eggs, and dairy products sold in American grocery chains and restaurants comes from animals raised in intensive-confinement systems (so-called factory farms) that impose significant stress on the animals in pursuit of efficiency. The result is that living creatures are often being treated as biological "machines."

The Humane Society of the United States promotes eating with conscience and embracing the Three **Rs**:

- **Reducing** the consumption of meat and other animal-based foods

- **Refining** the diet by avoiding products from the worst production systems (e.g., switching to cage-free eggs)

- **Replacing** meat and other animal-based foods in the diet with plant-based foods

How are the "Three Rs" similar to or different from the guidelines presented in the Talmud?

_____

_____

_____

_____

_____

Food Fact:

Some Jews today subscribe to a way of eating known as "**MOOSHY**," which means "**M**eat **O**nly **O**n **S**habbat, **H**appy occasions, and *Yom tov* (holidays)."

What Do You Think?

Jewish tradition supports both the eating of meat and vegetarian eating. Here are three different views:

Rav Avraham Kook

Rav Avraham Kook (1865–1935), the first Ashkenazic chief rabbi of Palestine, thought that in an ideal world everyone would be vegetarian, and that God's permission to eat meat was only a temporary concession. But he himself famously ate a small amount of chicken every Shabbat, perhaps to acknowledge that we are not yet living in a perfect world.

Moses Maimonides

Moses Maimonides (1135–1204), rabbi, doctor, and philosopher, believed that it was important to treat animals raised for food with respect since animals feel physical and emotional pain. Yet, Maimonides still taught that a balanced diet, which included meat, was the most healthful and the most advisable.

Rabbi Katy Allen

Today, **Rabbi Katy Allen** and **Rabbi Fred Scherlinder Dobb** advocate for a vegetarian diet they call a "new kosher." Because of how factory-farmed animals are raised, and because of environmental concerns, they argue that only vegetarian foods are "fit to eat."

Split into three different groups corresponding to each of the Jewish viewpoints above. Collaborate with your group, and prepare and present a defense of your rabbi's position.

Rabbi Fred Scherlinder Dobb

Takeaway Jewish tradition offers powerful resources that allow us to reflect on meat eating today, but we have to apply that knowledge to a farming system that is vastly different from biblical and Talmudic times. There are many authentically Jewish ways to approach eating animals—from eating meat with a few restrictions to eating no meat at all.

To Select
Kashrut

Jewish tradition has a set of guidelines and wise advice about what we put in our bodies. These practices touch on a variety of different issues—caring for animals, eating meat, cleanliness, and community, among others. Today, many people call these practices *kashrut,* from the word *kasher,* which literally means "fit [to eat]." *Kashrut* means different things to different people.

What Does "Fit to Eat" Mean to You?

Write down three foods you consider fit to eat and three foods you consider not fit to eat, and your reasons:

Fit to Eat	Not Fit to Eat	Why?
1.	1.	1.
2.	2.	2.
3.	3.	3.

The Laws of *Kashrut*

The laws of *kashrut* are based on texts that appear in the Torah. The following are some of the requirements for animals to be considered kosher:

Fish that have fins and scales

Animals that chew their cud and have split hooves, like cows, sheep, and goats

Birds that are not birds of prey (birds that eat other animals)

Beyond a list of animals one can and cannot eat, meat must be prepared in a specific way in order to be considered kosher. Slaughter must be done by a *shochet,* someone trained in the act of slaughter and the laws surrounding the act. This person is with the animal in its final moments, ensuring a human connection to the animal, and inspects the animal to make sure it was in good health. In addition, milk and meat are eaten separately, and blood, the life essence of an animal, must be drained from the animal before eating it.

What are some rules in your household and in your school? What do they limit?

_____

_____

Do you think the rules in your household are good ones? Which ones make sense to you?

_____

_____

_____

In Jewish tradition there are A LOT of rules about which foods are okay to eat and which foods are not—many more rules than there are about other topics. Why do you think there are so many rules?

_____

_____

_____

What makes a rule a good idea? As a class, write down the Ten Commandments of your classroom. Make five of them food related, and list those five here:

1. _____

2. _____

3. _____

4. _____

5. _____

Portrait of Maimonides,
19th century

Portrait of Nachmanides,
wall painting in Acre, Israel

Are You What You Eat?

Have you ever heard the phrase "You are what you eat"? What does this phrase mean to you? Do you think it refers to your body or your spirit? Below are two (of many) different understandings of the meaning behind the traditional *kashrut* guidelines. Which do you find meaningful? Divide into two groups, "body" and "spirit," and debate.

Maimonides (1135–1204) understood the dietary laws as a means of keeping the body healthy. He thought that the meat of forbidden animals, birds, and fish was unwholesome and indigestible.

Nachmanides (1194–1270) saw the dietary laws as beneficial to the spirit rather than the body. He observed that the forbidden animals and birds are predators, whereas the permitted animals are vegetarians, calmer and less violent creatures. Perhaps, he said, the character of the animals is transmitted through their flesh, so we should not eat predators.

Create Your Own *Hechsher*

One of the beautiful parts of *kashrut* is that it asks us to be intentional and thoughtful about what food and ingredients we eat.

A *hechsher* is a symbol or label that appears on food that tells the consumer that the food is kosher according to Jewish tradition. Here are some examples:

Above are labels that you might see on goods that signify that the food has been produced under specific conditions.

The standards of kosher certifications change as the way we eat in the modern world continues to change. Recently, additional certifications for kosher food have been introduced that take into account fair labor standards and ethical treatment of animals.

Food Fact:

The Fair Trade movement works to help farmers get fair pricing, and attain safe working conditions for food workers.

Organic means that food is grown without chemical fertilizers and pesticides.

Design a kosher certification label for a product that would alert customers to a food issue that is meaningful to you.

What environmental, ethical, and Jewish values would a farm or producer have to follow to get your certification? Write a checklist for how you would evaluate a product.

1. _____   4. _____

2. _____   5. _____

3. _____   6. _____

Takeaway Kosher literally means "fit [to eat]." Many Jews around the world make decisions about what they eat based on many principles, including traditional kosher laws, agricultural practices, and trade issues. It is up to each of us to decide what is and is not "fit to eat."

To Eat
Blessing the Meal

Have you ever thought about the best way to say "thank you" for your food? Do you think it makes more sense to give thanks before or after you eat—or both? In Jewish tradition, some people offer blessings of thanks before they eat. There is also a tradition of saying "thanks" again after we've eaten, with *Birkat Hamazon*.

Blessings before the Meal

Below is a list of traditional Jewish blessings that are recited before eating different foods. Draw a line from the blessing to the photo of the food for which it expresses thanks.

בָּרוּךְ אַתָּה, יְיָ אֱלֹהֵינוּ, מֶלֶךְ הָעוֹלָם,
הַמּוֹצִיא לֶחֶם מִן הָאָרֶץ.

Praised are You, Adonai Our God, Ruler of the world, who brings forth bread from the earth.

בָּרוּךְ אַתָּה, יְיָ אֱלֹהֵינוּ, מֶלֶךְ הָעוֹלָם,
בּוֹרֵא מִינֵי מְזוֹנוֹת.

Praised are You, Adonai Our God, Ruler of the world, who creates different kinds of foods. (Used for grains other than bread.)

בָּרוּךְ אַתָּה, יְיָ אֱלֹהֵינוּ, מֶלֶךְ הָעוֹלָם,
בּוֹרֵא פְּרִי הַגָּפֶן.

Praised are You, Adonai Our God, Ruler of the world, who creates the fruit of the vine.

בָּרוּךְ אַתָּה, יְיָ אֱלֹהֵינוּ, מֶלֶךְ הָעוֹלָם,
בּוֹרֵא פְּרִי הָעֵץ.

Praised are You, Adonai Our God, Ruler of the world, who creates the fruit of the tree.

בָּרוּךְ אַתָּה, יְיָ אֱלֹהֵינוּ, מֶלֶךְ הָעוֹלָם,
בּוֹרֵא פְּרִי הָאֲדָמָה.

Praised are You, Adonai Our God, Ruler of the world, who creates the fruit of the earth.

בָּרוּךְ אַתָּה, יְיָ אֱלֹהֵינוּ, מֶלֶךְ הָעוֹלָם,
שֶׁהַכֹּל נִהְיָה בִּדְבָרוֹ.

Praised are You, Adonai Our God, Ruler of the world, whose words make all things come into being.
(Used for all other foods)

As you read the blessings, did they make sense to you? What questions do you have about them?

_____

_____

_____

Why do you think these were the blessings the ancient rabbis came up with?

_____

_____

_____

Why do you think the blessings thank God for trees, vines, and earth if the blessings are about foods?

_____

_____

_____

If you were to write your own blessing for your favorite food, what would you say?

_____

_____

_____

Blessings after the Meal

When we are hungry, it is easy to be thankful for food. It is when we have been satisfied that it is sometimes difficult to remember to be grateful.

When you have eaten your fill, give thanks to the Lord....
(Deuteronomy 8:10)

According to the Midrash, Moses wrote the first piece of the *Birkat Hamazon*, the traditional blessings after a meal, when he saw the manna fall for the first time. Imagine that you are in the middle of the wilderness after having fled from Egypt with only matzah to eat. What would you say after your first manna?

In groups of two or three, choose one person to be a television reporter who is interviewing one or two Israelites to get their reactions upon first receiving manna. If you have a video camera handy, you might even record your interviews!

From *The Israelites Collecting Manna from Heaven*, by Master of James IV of Scotland

Mindful Meditation

For some people, blessings help them have a greater appreciation for their food. Others find that blessings help them to eat more mindfully and savor every taste and smell and texture. To be "mindful" is to be very aware and to pay very close attention to everything around you. As an exercise, mindfulness is a practice of trying to be very aware of all the details of a situation.

This mindfulness eating exercise will help you to think about the taste, texture, and feel of a food; it gives you time to think about all the people and things that are required to get the food from the farm to your table.

For this activity, cut an apple into slices and choose one slice. Don't eat it yet!

Get comfortable. It's difficult to enjoy food if you're anxious or tense. Close your eyes, take a few deep breaths, get quiet, and notice how you feel inside. Let your thoughts just drift through your mind like clouds through the sky. Concentrate on each breath you take, the inhale and the exhale….

Open your eyes and look closely at your apple slice….

Notice its shape, its colors, its curves and undulations, all of its details….

Now smell your apple slice….

Now consider for a moment all of the people involved in getting this apple into your hand. Apple farmers, truck drivers, storekeepers, men and women…. Imagine how hard they are working to support themselves and their families….

Now consider all the ways in which nature has supported the creation of this apple by making fertile soil, clouds and rainwater, energy from sunshine, air….

Finally, think about the tree from which this apple grew. Think of the tree's roots reaching down into the soil, think of the strong trunk and rough bark, and think of the branches that stretch to the sky. Think of the whole tree….

Now, say the *bracha* and bless the fruit of the apple tree:

בָּרוּךְ אַתָּה, יְיָ אֱלֹהֵינוּ, מֶלֶךְ הָעוֹלָם, בּוֹרֵא פְּרִי הָעֵץ.

Baruch atah, Adonai Eloheinu, Melech ha'olam, borei pri ha'eitz.

Praised are You, Adonai Our God, Ruler of the world, who creates the fruit of the tree.

Now bite into the apple and take in the flavors.... Notice the physical sensations of chewing, the movements of your jaw.... Swallow your bite of apple and pay attention to the sensation of swallowing.... How far down your throat can you still feel the apple?

What did you notice about the apple?

_____

_____

Did this slice of apple taste different from other apples you have eaten in the past? Why or why not?

_____

_____

How would meals be different if you ate every food like this?

_____

_____

Takeaway There is much to be thankful for when it comes to the food on your plate. Jewish tradition provides one way of saying "thanks" both before and after eating, but there are many ways to honor and give gratitude for food.

Sharing Food

Millions of people around the world go hungry every day—yet enough food is actually produced to feed everyone. Judaism has a strong tradition—in fact, a requirement—of providing food for those in need, as well as sharing food and hospitality with guests.

Hunger and Food in America

- In America, 1 in 6 people face hunger. More than 1 in 5 children is at risk of hunger. Among African-Americans and Latinos, it's 1 in 3.

- 40% of food is thrown out in the US every year, or about $165 billion worth. All of this uneaten food could feed 25 million Americans.

- Over 20 million children receive free or reduced-price lunch each school day. Less than half of them get breakfast, and only 10% have access to summer meal sites.

Good Food Is Thrown Out for Many Reasons:

- Some of this food is thrown out by consumers who don't finish everything on their plates.

- Sometimes people throw out food that is still good to eat, but is past the expiration date listed on the label.

- Food is spoiled before it even gets to the consumer because of bad storage.

- Food is wasted before it even gets to the consumer because of inefficient transportation systems.

- Consumers expect and demand perfect-looking produce, so fruits and vegetables that are just slightly bruised are thrown away.

How does it make you feel to read these statistics?

_____

_____

Describe how you would feel if you were frequently hungry or often had to skip meals. Would it affect your schoolwork? Would your mood change?

_____

_____

Framing the Text

Open Your Doors

Sarah and Abraham Hosting Three Angels
by the Providence Lithograph Company

[Abraham] was sitting at the entrance of the tent as the day grew hot.
Looking up, he saw three men standing near him. As soon as he saw them,
he ran from the entrance of the tent to greet them and, bowing low to the ground, he said, "My lords, if it please you, do not go on past your servant. Let a little water be brought; bathe your feet and recline under the tree. And let me fetch a morsel of bread that you may refresh yourselves; then go on—seeing that you have come your servant's way....

Abraham hastened into the tent to Sarah, and said, "Quick, [get] three seahs of choice flour! Knead and make cakes!" Then Abraham ran to the herd, took a calf, tender and choice, and gave it to a servant-boy, who hastened to prepare it. [Abraham then] took curds and milk and the calf that had been prepared and set these before them; and he waited on them under the tree as they ate. (Genesis 18:1–8)

From this story, Abraham and Sarah became our models of how to be good hosts and how to treat those who are hungry. How can we be good hosts in our society today? Use the following chart to identify some aspects of being a good host, and what you can do to practice these values.

What makes a good host?	How can I practice this value?
1.	1.
2.	2.
3.	3.
4.	4.

Framing the Text

Because You Were Strangers

Read the texts below and answer the questions.

[…God befriends] the stranger, providing him with food and clothing. You too must befriend the stranger, for you were strangers in the Land of Egypt.
(Deuteronomy 10:18–19)

When you give food to a hungry person, give him your best and sweetest food.
(Maimonides, *Mishneh Torah*, 7:11)

When you reap the harvest of your land, you shall not reap all the way to the edges of your field, or gather the gleanings of your harvest. You shall not pick your vineyard bare, or gather the fallen fruit of your vineyard; you shall leave them for the poor and the stranger….
(Leviticus 19:9–10)

If…there is a needy person among you, one of your kinsmen in any of your settlements in the land that the Lord your God is giving you, do not harden your heart and shut your hand against your needy kinsman. Rather you must open your hand and lend him sufficient for whatever he needs. (Deuteronomy 15:7–8)

If a stranger comes and says, "I am hungry. Please give me food," we are not allowed to check to see if he is honest or not; we must immediately give him food. (Maimonides, *Mishneh Torah* 6:6)

When you are asked in the world to come, "What was your work?" and you answer, "I fed the hungry," you will be told, "This is the gate of the Lord, enter into it, you who have fed the hungry." (*Midrash Psalms* 118:17)

DONATION BOX

FOOD DONATIONS

Which approach to giving food to the hungry do you prefer? Why?

_____

_____

_____

_____

Which of these texts stand out to you? Which challenge you? Why?

_____

_____

_____

_____

Why do you think food is at the center of all these sources? Why not shelter or clothing?

_____

_____

_____

_____

Play Jacob and Esau

Read the following verses, then split into groups to act out this scene.

> When the boys grew up, Esau became a skillful hunter, a man of the outdoors; but Jacob was a mild man who stayed in camp. Isaac favored Esau because he had a taste for game; but Rebekah favored Jacob. Once when Jacob was cooking a stew, Esau came in from the open, famished. And Esau said to Jacob, "Give me some of that red [stew] to gulp down, for I am famished!"... Jacob said, "First sell me your birthright." And Esau said, "I am at the point of death, so of what use is my birthright to me?" But Jacob said, "Swear to me first." So [Esau] swore to him, and sold his birthright to Jacob. Jacob then gave Esau bread and lentil stew; he ate and drank, and he rose and went away.... (Genesis 25:27–34)

What do you think about how Jacob and Esau acted in this situation? What do you think influenced how each of them acted? Did either act unfairly?

_____

_____

Can you remember a time when you were very hungry? What did it feel like? Did it make you act differently than you normally do?

_____

_____

Esau Sells His Birthright for Potage of Lentils by Gerard Hoet

Local Research

Many people today rely on emergency food providers (EFPs) for their next meal. EFPs can range from a soup kitchen, where hot meals are served, to food banks, where dry and fresh foods are distributed. Many EFPs rely on volunteers for help packing, cooking, and distributing meals.

Imagine that you are in charge of recruiting food bank volunteers. It is your job to send out an e-mail to the people in your community asking them to help.

Before you design your e-mail blast, go online and find a food bank or soup kitchen in your area. What would you like people to know about the work the organization does, and what would you be looking for in a volunteer? What kind of work would a volunteer do, and what can he or she expect to learn or gain from the experience? Did you learn anything through your research that surprised you?

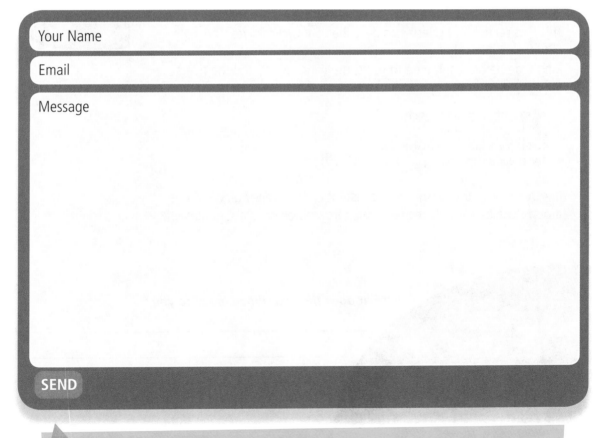

Your Name

Email

Message

SEND

Takeaway Farms currently produce enough food to feed everyone, and yet many people still go hungry around the world. We must place the responsibility to end world hunger on people—on ourselves—by learning to share our food with our own neighbors.

How often do you throw things in the garbage can each day? Which things do you most often throw away? How many of them could be reduced, reused, or recycled? In Jewish tradition, the value of *bal tashchit*—do not destroy or waste—challenges the Jewish people to sustain the earth by making as few trips to the garbage can as possible. In exploring the idea of *bal tashchit*, you will learn how to reduce, reuse, and recycle from a Jewish perspective.

Framing the Text

To Everything There Is a Season

This first section of Ecclesiastes describes our cyclical lives. The author proclaims that everything that exists today has existed for a long time before us: The earth turns, the winds blow, and the rivers flow: "There is nothing new under the sun."

> All streams flow into the sea,
> Yet the sea is never full;
> To the place [from] which they flow
> The streams flow back again. (Ecclesiastes 1:7)

In other words, the earth is in a constant cycle of renewal. What goes around comes around, and what we throw away does not go away.

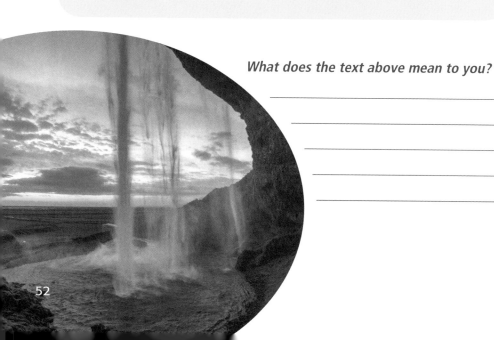

What does the text above mean to you?

_____

_____

_____

_____

_____

The Water Cycle

The water cycle describes the continuous movement of water above, on, and below the surface of the earth. Water is able to move in this cycle by changing states between liquid, vapor, and ice.

Apples are made up of about 85 percent water. The water in the apples you eat may have fallen as rain halfway around the world last year before making its way up the roots of an apple tree into that apple.

The same water in the apples you eat might have been used one hundred million years ago by a dinosaur!

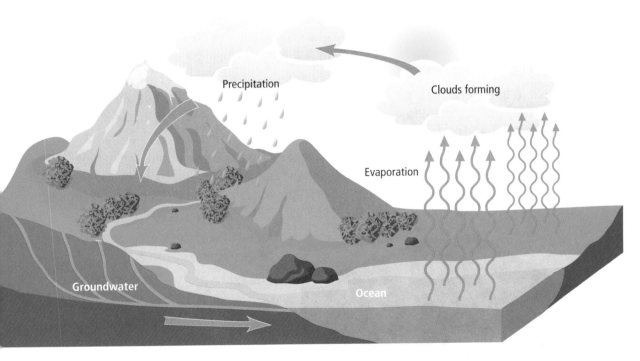

What are some actions that people can do to be a part of earth's natural cycles?

_____

_____

Compost and the Cycle of Life

Composting is a system by which people use microorganisms to decompose organic matter—like kitchen scraps or fallen leaves—and turn it into fertilizer. In this cycle, the food we eat today is recycled into fertilizer for the food we'll eat tomorrow, instead of going to a landfill.

Composting is based on the nutrient cycle, the process in the natural world by which dead plant and animal matter is decomposed, released as nutrients into the soil, then taken in by plants, which are eaten by animals, beginning the cycle again. While composting happens on very large scales, people can also compost in their own backyards.

Freeze!

When we throw out organic matter instead of composting it, we break the chain of the nutrient cycle. Without the nutrient cycle, the natural world would come to a standstill, as this game of freeze tag will show.

Split up into three groups: Organic Matter (food scraps and waste, leaves and grass clippings), Decomposers (fungus, bacteria, and invertebrates, like worms, that live in the soil), and Garbage Collectors. Feel free to really get into character!

In this game of freeze tag, the Organic Matter must get to the Decomposers before the Garbage Collectors come. When Organic Matter and Decomposers are tagged by the Garbage Collectors, they must freeze. To unfreeze, a Decomposer needs to come along and tag Organic Matter and other Decomposers back into the game.

Once all the Decomposers are frozen, the game comes to an end.

Now, run!

When you have completed the game, discuss as a class: What would happen in the natural world if there were no more decomposers? What would a forest look like? What would your backyard look like?

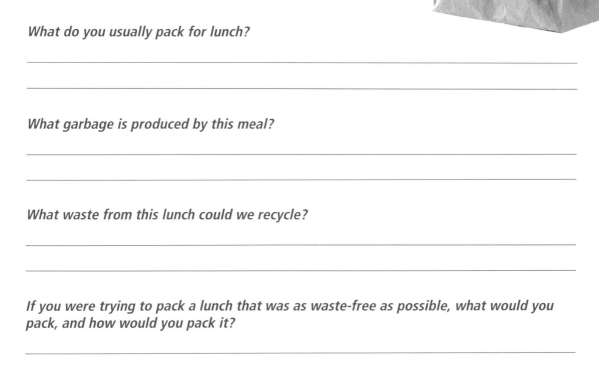

What's for Lunch?

Small changes we make in our lives can make a big difference in the world. The lunches we bring to school every day can help us practice the values we've been exploring.

What do you usually pack for lunch?

_____

_____

What garbage is produced by this meal?

_____

_____

What waste from this lunch could we recycle?

_____

_____

If you were trying to pack a lunch that was as waste-free as possible, what would you pack, and how would you pack it?

_____

_____

Vote and Take Action!

In the space below, create a campaign poster for a new *bal tashchit* practice you think your class should adopt. Be sure to include three steps that need to be taken to make the practice happen, including who will take on the project after you. Share your poster and ideas with the class, then vote as a class on what new conservation practices you want to adopt. Work together to make a plan for how you would make this happen. What would success look like?

Framing the Text

Bal Tashchit

The Jewish prohibition against wasting comes from Deuteronomy. Many people use this passage as the basis for a Jewish environmental ethic.

When in your war against a city you have to besiege it a long time in order to capture it, you must not destroy its [fruit] trees, wielding the ax against them. You may eat of them, but you must not cut them down.... (Deuteronomy 20:19)

In wartime, destruction is part of everyday life. Why is this passage especially powerful in that context?

_____

_____

_____

What habits could you change in order to protect the natural world?

_____

_____

_____

Takeaway The Jewish calendar operates in cycles. On some days we fast, and on some we feast. There are days we work, and days we rest. We celebrate good times and remember bad times. There are times of destruction, and times of renewal.

The earth operates in cycles, as well. When we observe *bal tashchit,* we need to be aware not just of reducing harm, but also of ensuring that earth's cycles remain in motion through reusing and recycling. Making sure that these cycles are vibrant and strong will make the earth a healthier and more sustainable place for ourselves and for all people.

To Sustain
Caring for Our Bodies

Jewish tradition teaches us that a spark of God lives inside each person. In the Torah we read that each human being is created in the image of God, *b'tzelem Elohim*. For this reason, Jewish tradition has a lot to say about how we care for ourselves—physically and spiritually. The idea of *shmirat haguf,* the obligation to care for our bodies, is seen as a way to honor God.

One important way that we care for our bodies is by thinking about what food we eat. Think about what you ate for breakfast or lunch today. How much of it came straight from the earth?

List three things you do to care for your body.

1. _____ 2. _____ 3. _____

Why do you do these things?

_____

Framing the Text

Created in God's Image

Rabbi Simcha Bunem of Przysucha is said to have carried a slip of paper in each of his pockets. One slip of paper read, "I am but dust and ashes"; the other, "For my sake the world was created." These two texts remind us that, on the one hand, we are very, very small in the scale of the universe, with bodies that get sick and are easily hurt; on the other hand, we are all unique, and we all have the power to create real change in the world.

The Torah teaches us that though we are human, we are also created in God's image:

> And God created man in [God's] image, in the image of God, [God] created man; male and female [God] created them. (Genesis 1:27)

What does it mean that we were created in God's image? Do you think this verse relates to one of Rabbi Bunem's slips of paper more than the other?

_____

_____

How can we treat our bodies in a way that recognizes we were made in God's image? How should we care for ourselves and our bodies?

_____

_____

Framing the Text

Eating in Moderation

Maimonides was both a doctor and a rabbi. He wrote extensively about health—how a person should care for his or her body.

> One should never eat unless one is hungry, nor drink unless one is thirsty....(Maimonides, *Mishneh Torah, Hilchot Dei'ot* 4:1–2)

How would you describe Maimonides's attitude toward food?

_____

_____

Do you think following his advice is easy or difficult? Why?

_____

_____

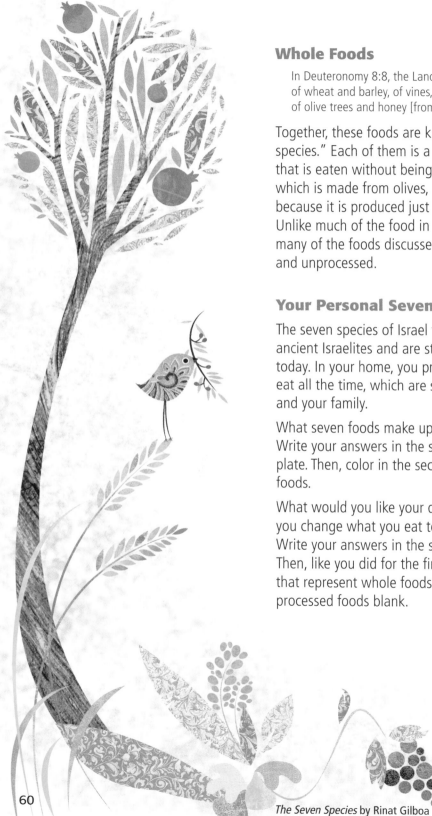

Whole Foods

In Deuteronomy 8:8, the Land of Israel is described as "a land of wheat and barley, of vines, figs, and pomegranates, a land of olive trees and honey [from dates]."

Together, these foods are known as the "seven species." Each of them is a "whole food," food that is eaten without being processed. Even olive oil, which is made from olives, is considered "whole" because it is produced just by squeezing olives. Unlike much of the food in our North American diet, many of the foods discussed in the Torah are whole and unprocessed.

Your Personal Seven Species

The seven species of Israel formed the basic diet of the ancient Israelites and are still important crops in Israel today. In your home, you probably have foods that you eat all the time, which are staples for you and your family.

What seven foods make up the majority of your diet? Write your answers in the seven sections of the green plate. Then, color in the sections that represent whole foods.

What would you like your diet to be, and how can you change what you eat to make it this way? Write your answers in the sections of the blue plate. Then, like you did for the first, color in the sections that represent whole foods. Leave the sections with processed foods blank.

The Seven Species by Rinat Gilboa

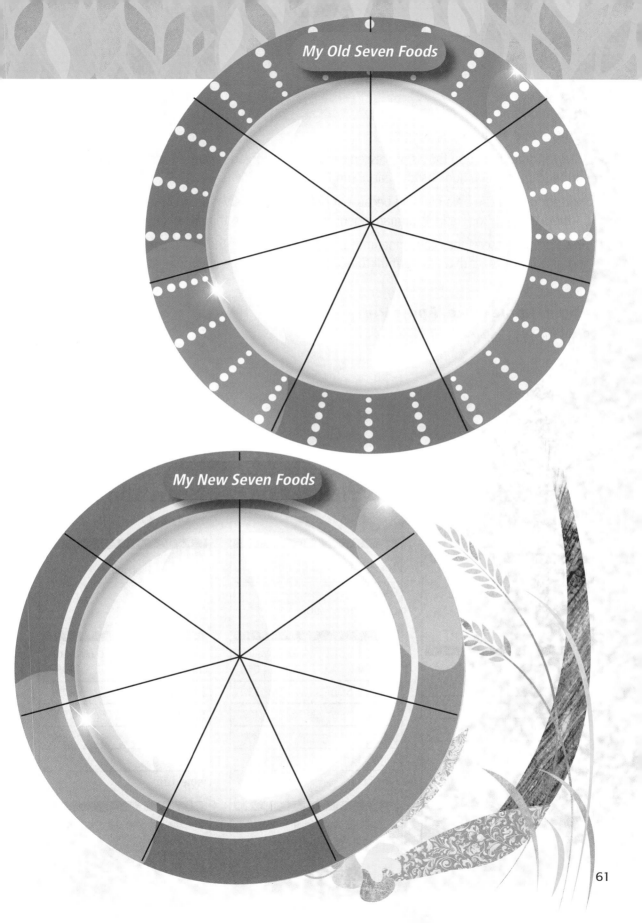

My Old Seven Foods

My New Seven Foods

61

Processed Foods

In Jewish tradition, food that is processed—like wine or bread—is often seen as a holy partnership between humans and earth and God.

Processing food can be a blessing because it helps with preservation, makes things edible, partners us with God, reflects human ingenuity, and can make things healthier.

However, processed foods can sometimes present a challenge. The process may be laborious and hide ingredients that are harmful to people, animals, or the environment.

Apple, Applesauce, Apple Pie

Read the food labels below.

Nutrition Facts

Serving Size 1 medium apple
(154g)

Amount Per Serving

Calories 80
Calories from Fat 0

	% Daily Value
Total Fat 0g	0%
Sodium 0mg	0%
Total Carbohydrate 22g	7%
Dietary Fiber 5g	20%
Sugars 16g	
Protein 0g	

Ingredients: apple

Nutrition Facts

Serving Size 1/2 Cup　(125g)

Amount Per Serving

Calories 80
Calories from Fat 0

	% Daily Value
Total Fat 0g	0%
Sodium 15mg	1%
Total Carbohydrate 15g	1%
Dietary Fiber 2g	8%
Sugars 11g	
Protein 0g	

Ingredients: apple, high fructose corn syrup, water, ascorbic acid

Nutrition Facts

Serving Size 1/8 of pie　(170g)

Amount Per Serving

Calories 80
Calories from Fat 0

	% Daily Value
Total Fat 8g	10%
Sodium 252mg	10%
Total Carbohydrate 75g	25%
Dietary Fiber 2g	8%
Sugars 52g	
Protein 3g	

Ingredients: flour, salt, shortening, water, sugar, cinnamon, nutmeg, apple, butter

Fill in the table below to record some of the differences between these items.

	Apple	Applesauce	Apple Pie
Number of ingredients			
Amount of fiber			
Serving size			
How do you serve each food?			
Can it be turned into another food?			
Does this food seem healthy?			

Which of these three are processed foods? Do you think there is such a thing as too much processing? Why or why not?

_____

_____

A Personal Commitment to Care for My Body

The American Academy of Pediatrics recommends the following healthy behaviors. You might already be doing some of them! Use the chart below to understand your own habits better, then answer the questions to create your own *shmirat haguf* commitment.

American Academy of Pediatrics Recommendations

	I already do this	I want to do this	I don't want to do this	To support this habit, I will . . .
Children and adults should eat at least 5 servings of fruits and vegetables daily.				
Limit your non-school related screen time (TV, video games, computer, etc.) to less than 2 hours per day.				
School-age youth need at least 60 minutes (1 hour) per day of moderate to vigorous activity, spread throughout the day.				
School age youth should not have sweetened drinks and sodas on most days.				
School age youth should have at least 8 hours of sleep every night.				

Make a Class Commitment

As a class, think of ways you can commit to a healthier lifestyle. Maybe you will all try to drink more water or bring in healthier snacks. The possibilities are endless!

List three suggestions for your class to consider:

1. _____

2. _____

3. _____

As a class, write your commitment on a poster board and have everyone sign it.

Takeaway Living a healthy life is about more than eating healthy foods and exercising. It can also have a spiritual element. By living a healthy life, you not only serve yourself, but your friends and family, too.

It's hard to live a healthy life on your own. Think about ways your family and friends can support your commitment and help you stick to it. Then, ask if they have a similar personal commitment, and support them.

To Sustain
Moderation

It sometimes is okay to indulge in lavish meals, like on special occasions and holidays. But it wouldn't be healthy to eat as if it were a holiday every day. Jewish tradition offers some guidance about how you can live your life with healthy moderation.

Relief of Assyrian warriors

Framing the Text

Overeating and Moderation

Sometimes, when we are under pressure, we make decisions without thinking about the consequences. Think about a time you might have made a poor eating decision by eating way too much or way too fast.

How did you feel afterward?

In the Book of Isaiah (22) we read about an act of great immoderation that happened before an impending raid on Jerusalem:

> As Assyrian chariots and armies filled the surrounding valleys, the people of Jerusalem knew that they were outnumbered and believed they would be overtaken the next morning. They wished to have a final meal, so they began slaughtering and eating their animals, and drinking wine. "Let us eat and drink; for tomorrow we shall die," they said. This act very much displeased God who reacted by saying, "Surely this iniquity shall not be forgiven till you die."

Why do you think God was so angry about this act of immoderation?

_____

_____

How were the people of Jerusalem affected by this act?

_____

_____

Who else (or what else) was affected by the act other than the people of Jerusalem?

_____

_____

How Much Is Too Much?

In an earlier chapter, we explored the challenges of world hunger. Now, we are exploring the opposite challenge, that of being surrounded by food and overindulgence. In our daily lives, most of us see food all around us, at grocery stores, in our homes, or in vending machines. But part of healthy eating, beyond the specific food choices we make, is knowing how much to eat and when to eat.

Modern medical studies have shown that overeating has a negative effect on our physical and emotional health. Jewish sages, too, wrote about this, hundreds of years ago.

More people die from overeating than from undernourishment. (Rabbi Nachman of Bratslav)

Work before eating; rest after eating. Do not eat ravenously, filling the mouth gulp after gulp without breathing space. (Maimonides)

How does your body feel when you've eaten enough?

_____

_____

_____

_____

Have you ever eaten too much food? Why? How did you feel while you were eating it? How did you feel afterward?

_____

_____

_____

_____

Sugar in Our World

Today we enjoy an abundance of food products, and they're available in all kinds of places—supermarkets, corner stores, farmers' markets, even gasoline stations. Many of these foods are filled with sugar. In small quantities, sugar is a necessary and healthy ingredient, but large amounts of sugar are not healthy for our bodies.

Divide into groups. Each group will receive one clear cup, a bowl of sugar, a teaspoon, and a soda nutrition facts label to analyze.

Step 1: Calculate the number of teaspoons of sugar in your soda by reading the label and following this formula:

Total grams of sugar divided by 4 = teaspoons of sugar in your food

If you drink an 8-ounce soda with 28 grams of sugar, how many teaspoons of sugar are you drinking? _____

If you drink a 12-ounce soda with 40 grams of sugar, how many teaspoons of sugar are you drinking? _____

If you drink a 20-ounce soda with 64 grams of sugar, how many teaspoons of sugar are you drinking? _____

Food Fact:

Kombucha is a drink made when bacteria and yeast are added to sugar and tea, then allowed to ferment. It's bright and fizzy, making it a great soda substitute.

Step 2: Measure out the number of teaspoons of sugar that are in your soda and pour them into a clear cup. Show your classmates how much sugar is in your drink.

Now take a look at some other drink labels, like juices, teas, and flavored waters. For each drink, note the number of grams of sugar it has. Fill out the chart by rating the amount of sugar in each drink as none, low, medium, or high. Then, for every drink, fill in how often you think one should drink this beverage.

1–10 grams sugar = Low

11–44 grams sugar = Medium

45+ grams sugar = High

Beverage	Amount of Sugar (None, Low, Medium, High)	How often should you drink this? (Every day, a few times a week, rarely)
Tap water	None (no sugar)	Every day

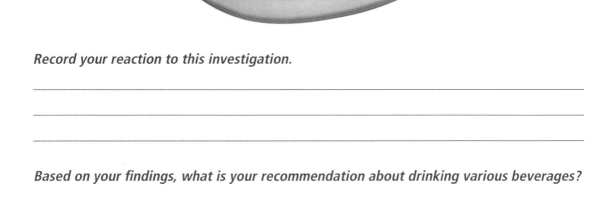

Record your reaction to this investigation.

_____

_____

_____

Based on your findings, what is your recommendation about drinking various beverages?

_____

_____

_____

Takeaway Jewish tradition encourages celebrating on special occasions! However, without us realizing it, more and more sugar has been added to common, everyday foods, leading to increased rates of obesity, diabetes, and heart disease. Now that you know how to calculate how much sugar is in foods and drinks, you can be a healthy consumer and figure out the best ways to celebrate in moderation.

Bringing It All Together

Throughout this course, we have learned about some of the Jewish perspectives on growing, harvesting, selecting, eating, and sustaining. We have learned that Jewish tradition not only provides us with a rich culinary background, but also with a way to live healthier, more sustainable lives.

Nutrition Facts—According to You!

If you were creating a nutrition label, but you could choose only five categories of information to include, what would they be? Make a list of your top five priorities (such as grams of fat, or origins of ingredients, or whether it's kosher), and what Jewish values relate to each of them.

Top Five Priorities	Jewish Values
1.	
2.	
3.	
4.	
5.	

What are some new things you have learned about the relationship between food and Jewish values and traditions?

_____

_____

Much of *Min Ha'aretz* is based on the work of Hazon,
an organization that works to creates healthier and more
sustainable communities in the Jewish world and beyond.

Hazon, the leading Jewish sustainability organization in
North America, stands at the forefront of a new Jewish food
movement. It combines the wisdom of ancient tradition with
contemporary knowledge about the environment to help guide
individuals, families, and communities to be stewards of the
earth and more educated, empowered consumers.

Learn more about Hazon's work at www.hazon.org.